D1603851

Sayings
of the
Sufi Sages

Compiled by
Lynn Wilcox, Ph. D.

M.T.O. SHAHMAGHSOUDI® PUBLICATIONS

Wilcox, Lynn (Ed.)

Sayings of the Sufi Sages

Copyright © 1997 by Maktab Tarighat Oveyssi Shahmaghsoudi (School of Islamic Sufism)®. All rights reserved – copyright throughout the world. No part of this publication may be reproduced, stored in a retrieval system, or transmitted in any form by any means without the express written consent of holder of copyright, the President of M.T.O. Shahmaghsoudi.

Library of Congress Catalog Card Number: 96-071230
ISBN: 0-910735-86-7

Printed in the U.S.A.

Published and distributed by M.T.O. Shahmaghsoudi
P.O. Box 5827
Washington, D.C. 20016
U.S.A.

website: http://mto.shahmaghsoudi.org

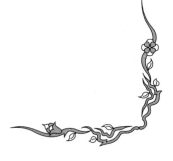

This volume is a selection of carefully chosen favorite quotations from works of the great Sufi Masters — the Spiritual Teachers of the 1,400 year old School of Sufism. Every statement is a distillation of an inspired essential concept. Chosen from works of poetry and prose, they provide a glimpse of the boundless knowledge, purity, truth and love with which these enlightened mystics guide sincere seekers.

Powerful antidotes to the apathy, conflict and dissatisfaction of modern life, they are filled with joy, hope, peace and love.

the sages...
peace be upon them

the sayings...

Keep watch over your heart.

Molana-al-Moazam
Hazrat Oveys Gharani

Whoever sets right his inward self, God sets right his outward self.

Amir-al-Moemenin Ali

If a person has a good idea about you, make his idea come true.

Amir-al-Moemenin Ali

He who corrects the way between himself and God, God shall correct his relationship with others.

Amir-al-Moeminin Ali

Since I have
domesticated
the wolf
of my soul,
everything
in the world
is at peace
with me.

Hazrat Abu Salim Habib
-ibn Moussa Zeyd Rai

*Remember God
and reject the
crowd.*

Hazrat Soltan
Ebrahim Adham

If you desire
well being,

renounce

worldly

attachments...

Sheikh Abu Solaiman
Davoud al-Ta'i

Do not say anything until you see it worth saying.

Sheikh Abu Ali
Shaghigh Balkhi

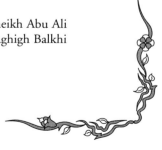

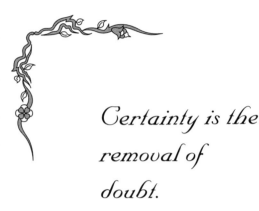

Certainty is the removal of doubt.

Abul Qasim
Muhammad al-Junayd

*They do not
know what they
do…*

Husayn ibn
Mansur al-Hallaj

*Enthusiasm is
the result of
affection;
whoever loves
Him is eager to
see Him.*

Sheikh Abu Bakr Dolaf
ibn Jahdar al-Shebli

Believers shall see with the light of the heart that which the naked eye is unable to see.

Sheikh Morshed abu-Ishaq
Shahriar Kazerouni

No blessing
arises from
anything in
which selfish
interest has a
part.

Ali b. Uthman al-Jullabi
al-Hujwiri

Put not your hope in people, for you will be wounded. Put your hope in God...

Abu-Isma'il Abdullah Ansari

*Do not brand as
false what you
are unable to
comprehend.*

Abu Hamid al-Ghazali

Be well-disposed toward your friend and your foe... with dignity free of pride and modesty short of abasement.

Abu Hamid al-Ghazali

*In all your
dealings take
the middle way,
for both
extremes of
conduct are
blameworthy.*

Abu Hamid al-Ghazali

Form and
attributes are
the niche and
glass from
which the light
of essence
shines.

Sheikh Hakim Sinai

Love's

conqueror is he

whom love

conquers.

Sheikh Hakim Sinai

*At the gate of
the King, a
beggar asks for
bread...
but the lover
desires food for
his soul.*

Sheikh Hakim Sinai

The seeing soul
perceives the
folly of praising
other than the
Creator.

Sheikh Hakim Sinai

*The Essence
of the First
Absolute
Light, God,
gives constant
illumination...*

Shihabuddin Yahya
Suhrawardi

Fear God and

none other.

Abdul-Qadir al-Jilani

Your heart is a
polished mirror.
You must wipe
it clean of the
veil of dust
which has
gathered
upon it.

Abdul-Qadir al-Jilani

If the magnet
were not loving,
how could it
attract the iron
with such
longing?

Ilyas ibn Yusuf Nizami

*All that you
have heard or
seen or known is
not even the
beginning of
what you must
know.*

Farid ud-Din Attar

Everyone's journey is toward his perfection. Everyone's proximity is according to his "state".

Farid ud-Din Attar

Seek the trunk
of the tree, and
do not worry
about whether
the branches do
or do not exist.

Farid ud-Din Attar

*Hope is the
remedy for
sorrow and fear
the rival of
action.*

Sheikh Najmeddin Kobra

Wherever there
is a ruin, there
is hope for a
treasure.

Molana Jalaluddin Rumi
(Molavi)

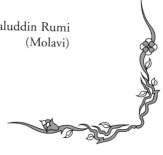

*The sea will
be the sea,
whatever the
drop's
philosophy.*

Molana Jalaluddin Rumi
(Molavi)

The Spirit has
no association
with man or
woman. It is
higher than
masculine or
feminine.

Molana Jalaluddin Rumi
(Molavi)

Whoever travels without a guide needs two hundred years for a two days' journey.

Molana Jalaluddin Rumi
(Molavi)

The reality of
hope is the joy
that comes with
awareness of
God's grace.

Sheikh Safieddin Ardebili

The one who
goes on this
journey on his
own will drown
in the mirage of
the self.

Sheikh Safieddin Ardebili

*In their
learned books
thou'lt seek in
vain the key to
Love's locked
gateway.*

Shamsuddin
Muhammad Hafiz

Go and do good.

Shamsuddin
Muhammad Hafiz

The perfect man is a copy of God.

Abu l-Karim ibn
Ibrahim al-Jili

'Tis folly to
pursue a host of
loves; a single
heart can but
one love
contain!

Nur-ud-Din
'Abd-Ur-Rahman Jami

The forms
which clothe
existence only
stay one moment
...in the next
they pass away.

Nur-ud-Din
'Abd-Ur-Rahman Jami

The wine of love shall awaken you to the mysteries of the heart.

Sheikh Amili Mohammad
B. Husain Baha Al Din

The drop loses its limitations when it falls into the boundless ocean.

Shah Ghasen Feizbakhsh

Man is an unusual
and amazing weave
of angel and beast.
Whenever he turns
to the beastly he is
less than the beast,
and whenever he
turns to the heavenly
he exceeds the angel.

Hadj Molla Hadi Sabzevari

*The science of
love cannot be
perceived.*

Molana-al-Moazam
Hazrat Jalaleddin Ali
Mir Abolfazl Angha

*Our duty, if we want
to understand sublime
matters, is to connect
ourselves to a person
who is higher than
others — more
enlightened, so as to
benefit from the
reflections of his
heart.*

Molana-al-Moazam
Hazrat Mir Ghotbeddin
Mohammad Angha

48

Unfulfilled souls mistake their creations for the truths of life.

Molana-al-Moazam
Hazrat Shah Maghsoud
Sadegh Angha

Whatever

appears to you

as the reality of

"self" is but one

stage ...

Molana-al-Moazam
Hazrat Shah Maghsoud
Sadegh Angha

Words do not convey the meaning.

Molana-al-Moazam
Hazrat Shah Maghsoud
Sadegh Angha

Do not leave me
unto myself, but
guide me to the
glory within,
and touch me
with Your
supreme
kindness.

Molana-al-Moazam
Hazrat Shah Maghsoud
Sadegh Angha

The ascent of man lies in his effort, as the flight of the bird depends on its wings...

Molana-al-Moazam
Hazrat Shah Maghsoud
Sadegh Angha

Study yourself ...the thing that attracts you the most is what possesses you.

Molana-al-Moazam
Hazrat Shah Maghsoud
Sadegh Angha

*The inspiring
sound of the
Timeless
Player makes
my heart
rejoice every
new day.*

Molana-al-Moazam
Hazrat Shah Maghsoud
Sadegh Angha

Reasoning can never manifest the truth... Truth must be seen.

Molana-al-Moazam
Hazrat Shah Maghsoud
Sadegh Angha

Words are the veils of truth.

Molana-al-Moazam
Hazrat Shah Maghsoud
Sadegh Angha

Tending the horse is to enable the rider to reach his destination.

Molana-al-Moazam
Hazrat Shah Maghsoud
Sadegh Angha

*The wise knows
that he does not
know and the
foolish does not.*

Molana-al-Moazam
Hazrat Shah Maghsoud
Sadegh Angha

Balance is the way of God and the way of the wise.

Molana-al-Moazam
Hazrat Shah Maghsoud
Sadegh Angha

*Make the best
of what has
been given you.*

Molana-al-Moazam
Hazrat Shah Maghsoud
Sadegh Angha

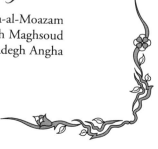

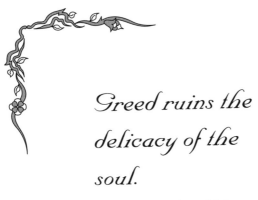

Greed ruins the delicacy of the soul.

Molana-al-Moazam
Hazrat Shah Maghsoud
Sadegh Angha

*Doubts are
what keep true
happenings out
of sight.*

Molana-al-Moazam
Hazrat Shah Maghsoud
Sadegh Angha

Those aware of
their poverty
shall receive
wealth.

Molana-al-Moazam
Hazrat Shah Maghsoud
Sadegh Angha

If we look closely, the underlying reason for all struggles is the attainment of tranquillity — each and everyone wants true tranquillity.

Molana-al-Moazam
Hazrat Shah Maghsoud
Sadegh Angha

*The storm of
the waters is of
greater
intensity at the
shores than at
the ocean
depths.*

Molana-al-Moazam
Hazrat Shah Maghsoud
Sadegh Angha

*The wise are
those who
acquire benefits
and repel losses.*

Molana-al-Moazam
Hazrat Shah Maghsoud
Sadegh Angha

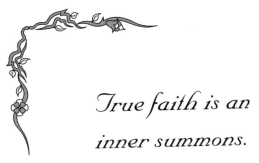

True faith is an

inner summons.

Molana-al-Moazam
Hazrat Shah Maghsoud
Sadegh Angha

*No one can
know you the
way you know
yourself.*

Molana-al-Moazam
Hazrat Shah Maghsoud
Sadegh Angha

*Time is short
and the day of
judgment is
near.*

Molana-al-Moazam
Hazrat Shah Maghsoud
Sadegh Angha

Desire is a
natural
tendency in life,
but pursuing it
distances you
farther from
life.

Molana-al-Moazam
Hazrat Shah Maghsoud
Sadegh Angha

*Real lovers are
not diverted by
the colors of the
world; they are
judged
according to
their patience.*

Molana-al-Moazam
Hazrat Shah Maghsoud
Sadegh Angha

*The delicate
have greater
endurance than
the harsh.*

Molana-al-Moazam
Hazrat Shah Maghsoud
Sadegh Angha

In awe and
silence,
in solitude of
heart,
are mysteries
revealed to the
sincere heart.

Molana Hazrat Salaheddin
Ali Nader Shah Angha

The true
meaning of
peace refers to
the inner
freedom and
spiritual
elevation of
each individual.

Molana Hazrat Salaheddin
Ali Nader Shah Angha

There is no
"I", only He
is the One -
unique. Let
this bright
reality shine
through to you.

Molana Hazrat Salaheddin
Ali Nader Shah Angha

*Goodness is the
seed of truth
and purity.*

Molana Hazrat Salaheddin
Ali Nader Shah Angha

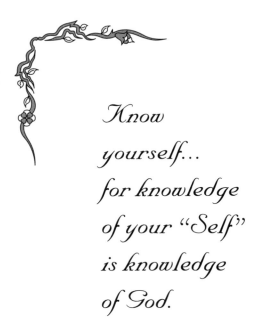

*Know
yourself...
for knowledge
of your "Self"
is knowledge
of God.*

Molana Hazrat Salaheddin
Ali Nader Shah Angha

*In the realm
of God…gender,
class, race,
ethnicity, etc.,
have no
relevance.*

Molana Hazrat Salaheddin
Ali Nader Shah Angha

*The mind knows
not how His
wondrous work
is done; in the
Hands of Love,
submit fully
your heart.*

Molana Hazrat Salaheddin
Ali Nader Shah Angha

*Mistake not a
mirage for the
Water of Life.*

Molana Hazrat Salaheddin
Ali Nader Shah Angha

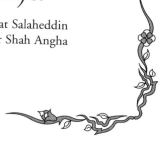

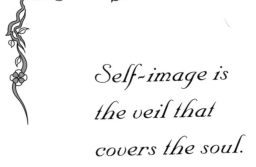

*Self-image is
the veil that
covers the soul.*

Molana Hazrat Salaheddin
Ali Nader Shah Angha

*Outer calmness
is the reflection
of inner
awareness.*

Molana Hazrat Salaheddin
Ali Nader Shah Angha

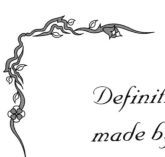

Definitions made by the senses do not speak of life's true essence.

Molana Hazrat Salaheddin
Ali Nader Shah Angha

Repentance is to part from all but God, and to see His Face with the inner eyes of your soul.

Molana Hazrat Salaheddin
Ali Nader Shah Angha

The heavens
listen to the
heart-wishes of
the sincere.

Molana Hazrat Salaheddin
Ali Nader Shah Angha

The joy that is
gained through
cognition and
love, can never
by ritual or
duty be gained.

Molana Hazrat Salaheddin
Ali Nader Shah Angha

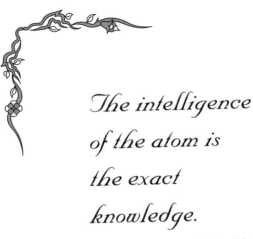

The intelligence
of the atom is
the exact
knowledge.

Molana Hazrat Salaheddin
Ali Nader Shah Angha

He who calls to
God from the
depths of his
heart, will find
his abode in the
clear skies of
love.

Molana Hazrat Salaheddin
Ali Nader Shah Angha

For the world to be redeemed from its current state, the Commandment of the Holy Prophet Moses, "Love thy neighbor," must be followed.

Molana Hazrat Salaheddin
Ali Nader Shah Angha

Man can be
cured of his
deep-rooted
illnesses by the
hands of the
Divine Healer.

Molana Hazrat Salaheddin
Ali Nader Shah Angha

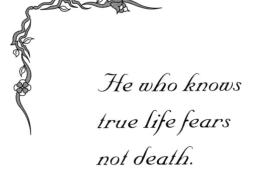

*He who knows
true life fears
not death.*

Molana Hazrat Salaheddin
Ali Nader Shah Angha